Meat Pie And Tatie Wine, Frikkies And Fries.

By the same author

A Voyage To Japanland

A Very Unprivate Private

At The Crooked Billet

Other Earths

From The Darkside Of The Fireplace

Love, Sex, Romance and Misadventure

My American Dreams

The Tackle (with Sue Houlston)

Meat Pie And Tatie Wine

I was born and lived in an East Riding village just before the end of the war. Shire horses still worked in the fields: most of the village men worked locally on one of the 14 farms: there were 3 shops, a butchers, joiner, and blacksmiths, a church, a chapel and even a village Drama Group. All in all a typical village of the time, in a time before a period of mad changes. As a boy I carried a .410 shotgun, not for sport, but to help feed us. Life was pleasant and quiet; by modern standards we were poor but we had all we needed.

I left the village in 1969 when I married. My mother left in the late 1970's, thus ending a family presence there traced back to around 1860. A very different village is still there, almost physically unchanged but bigger with once agricultural land now given over to housing, and at the most 3 working farms, no longer such a working farming village.

1950
Apples
Binder Band
Withernwick
Winter 1947
Tipper
Hooping Day
Forge Cottage circa 1950
Forge Cottage
High Street Granny
'Tatie Wine
Mam's Homemade Meat Pie
On a Winter's Saturday Night
Simple Tastes
The Death Of Poor Dicky Birds
Croftie's Barn
Billy Bulson's Farm
Bread
Fields
Germ Warfare Revisited
Special Place
Peaceful Place
Saturday Night, Yorkshire, 1960
Toast
Village Dance

Chawin' Baccy
Expansion
Great Aunt Ada
Memories
Conversations
Emily Medforth Village, School Teacher
Floods
Village Churchyard
Summer Childhood
Summer circa 1953
Rough Shooting 3
1957
Hornsea, 1954
Hunters' Moon
Conflicts
Just a Box of Old Photos
Friendships 1959

1950

a new decade
we had it made
the warring 40's past
at long long last
the sky was bluer
the world was newer
as a lad of 7
life was heaven
then the 50's passed

Apples

We picked apples, Uncle and me,
Balanced there in his apple tree.
I thought we were up so high
I could catch the pigeons flying by.

I was three, maybe four
Certainly not any more.
Later on when I grew tall
I knew we weren't so high at all.

But we picked apples, Uncle and me,
Balanced there in his apple tree.
I thought we were up so high
I could touch and stroke the sky.

Binder Band

We used to tie our keks with binder band
Both at the waist and at each knee
On a scale of one to ten
Not a modish sight to see;
But when we were threshing
We didn't think of that
Just that the binder band
Could stop an invading rat.
For when we were forking stooks
To the elevator from the stack
Nesting rats were liable to
Climb and bite and attack,
But a good length of binder band
Would keep the buggers out
As they flailed
And ran about

Until the terriers would catch 'em,
Maybe tear 'em to tatters,
Lovely dogs really
But really vicious ratters.
Country life
Was more simple then
Everything had
Its where and it's when.
You don't see many stacks these days

Nor so many farms for that matter;
Food all out of season tasteless,
It's cheaper and supposed to be better.
And you never see a threshing team
Touting for work about the land
And I wonder if you can still buy
Those huge great balls of binder band

Withernwick

in the village where I was born
there was always lots of trees
especially those in the church yard
gently swaying in the breeze
I suppose there must have been storms
when those branches swung and thrashed
and there must have been times
when branches split and smashed
but overhanging our cottage
those giants to my child's eyes
sent me to sleep
with their whispers and sighs.
and woke me in the morning
as they played along
to the chorus
of dawn bird song.

some carried my name
carved with my first knife
all boys had one then
part of country life.
I sheltered from rain under those trees
trunks tightly gripped between my knees
as tightly as I would later hold a lover
as I scrambled as high as I dared to look over
my world the village spread below

Most of those trees like my family
are now dead and gone
those that are left shelter the graves
for us survivors who've moved on.
I rarely go back now
I feel so alone
but I keep my memories
and the village keeps the bones
But over the years
It still calls to me
My wonderful village
Of singing trees.

Winter 1947

horses died that year, two great Shires
up to their shoulders in drifted snow
just yards away from stacked hay
yet yards too far for them to go;
so they stood shoulder to shoulder,
great sad eyes opened wide to stare
as if into distant worlds well beyond
the ken of any villager gathered there.
in sadness, yet in celebration
of a hard winter now broken.
these poor dead horses
a small reminder, a token
of the frailty of life,
of a winter's depth of power,
and soon to come a spring with
blossoms to burst into flower.
and we half forgot lanes blocked
by snow drifted hedge top high
and every single step taken an ache
to a cold leg and a straining thigh.
or walking between high stacked
white walls along paths dug and made
by aching arms and shoulders
wielding heavy digging spades.
it seemed to last forever in the village
then suddenly was almost gone

and the seasons in their turn
churned inexorably on.
and those poor dead Shire horses,
soon gone to the knackers' yard,
still drift back from childhood memories,
most remembered of a winter deep and hard.
my earliest retained memory
from life filled with joy
seen through the eyes of
a cold and crying boy,
and I still try to write about them
but somehow I can never find
words sufficiently fitting to describe
that scene burned deep in my mind.

Tipper

My dad just called him Tipper
So I just called him the same;
Must have been a few years
Before I really knew his name;
But there was always excitement
When Tipper appeared on the road
His. great blue Fordson tractors
Pulling their creaking convoy load

Into the stack yard of some farm
Everything cleared out of the way
For Tipper's gang and his equipment
To get an early start on threshing day.
The great driving belts of leather
Strung taut from tractor to machine
A dusty noisy busy working constant
Shifting changing moving scene

The terriers straining waiting
For the rats to leave the stacks
To fall prey to their vicious
Biting nipping killing attacks
And Tipper in the stackyard
Ever there in control
Making that hectic scene
Into a coherent whole

Sacks of corn being carried
Sacks of chaff being cleared
Stacks getting smaller
As the day's ending neared
Noise and dust and confusion
Then Tipper was away
Gone maybe a year
Until next threshing day

Hooping Day'.

Early memories, being strapped in my pram
After a good tanning from an angry mam;
The snows of Forty Seven when the Shires died;
Billy Bulson's farm and my only Shire ride;
Hooping day in the blacksmiths yard
When Owen and uncle worked so hard

Checking and balancing each wheel's trim
Before replacing each wheel's worn metal rim.
There was this big cast plate on the ground
With a ring of braziers circled around.
At the centre of the plate, at the very nub
Was a hole to accommodate each wood hub.

You could feel the heat, each brazier red,
As each hoop was lowered into its bed
Where it would expand so it would slip
Around a wheel rim to shrink and grip.
Each was doused to speed the cold
And so increase the tight firm hold.

They worked the whole day
That was the only possible way
Each wagon was ready for the fields
To transport that year's harvest yield.
After school we kids watched, standing around
Well out of the way of the working ground.

If any kid got a bit too near
Uncle or Owen would clip an ear.
That was in the years after the war
Five or six at the most, certainly no more,
Before Fordson and Fergies finally ousted shires
And metal rims were replaced by pneumatic tyres.

Close my eyes and I can hear the sounds
Of iron shod wooden wheels booling the ground:
Open my eyes and it's a whole world away,
Slower, gentler, nicer perhaps, than today.
Sometime I think now I understand why
Old people accept when it's their time to die.
Without a single kick or scream
Just slipping away into their dreams.

Forge Cottage circa 1950

The smith yard, the smithy yard
Such a place of joy;
A paradise really
For a growing, curious boy.

There was usually one corn Binder
Waiting in the forge yard for repair,

But to me that rusty old machine,
Parked so invitingly just there
Was the stuff of my dreams,
For it became my sailing ship;
And I sat high on its metal seat
Planning my exploratory trip.

Or I could slip down deep inside
And it became that special place
Where I planned my journeys
Into outer deep deepest space.
Down there in my engine room
Plotting routes for yonder star,
In my imagination that old binder
Kept me near yet took me so very far.

I made so many journeys
To cities not yet known,
And people and places
On charts not yet shown.
And yet always there to hear
No matter where I chose to roam
Those Blacksmith hammer's sounds
Reassuringly marking my way home.

The smith yard, the smithy yard
Such a place of joy;
A paradise really
For a growing, curious boy.

Forge Cottage, Withernwick

I loved those old cart horse Shires,
big and solid and calm
Billy Bulson let me ride one once
'tatie picking on his farm;
And when Uncle Wilf would shoe them.
We'd hear the clip clop
Of hooves across the yard
towards his blacksmith's shop.

They'd duck their heads through the door and once inside
Stand there patiently as their halter rope was tied
To one of those special rings set deep in the forge brick.
Uncle would approach them slowly then, part of the trick
To keep them from fretting under the low dark roof.
Firmly grasping a fetlock then to raise a large hoof
Which he would cradle between two bent knees
Held firmly there so he could work at his ease
Cutting, filing and shaping ready for each shoe
So that each was fitted perfectly, firm and true.
I can't forget the smell as the shoe, still hot
Was laid in place to sear its own right spot

Then deftly nailed and then
The process repeated over again
Till each old shoe
Replaced with new.
So many times I stood there as a little boy,
Scenes I recall with so much sheer joy.

That world is gone, those times near dead
Except I store them safely here in my head.
Forge Cottage is now a weekend retreat
And Uncle's yard once clean and neat
Is full of rampant weeds.
The Forge remains, a building preserved.
With its long village history
The very least it, and the past, deserved.

High Street Granny

High Street Granny Barker, diabetic and stout
Didn't have enough agility to get out and about
Except to her back way to bring cold water in
Pumped by hand from a deep clear spring.
For she had a lifelong hobby as most folk do
This spring water made wicked home brew;
Potato Whiskey, Beer, Marrow Rum, Wine
Most vegetables or fruit would do just fine.

I remember once a tasting to see if I liked
And on the way home falling off my bike.
As for maturing it didn't take too long
And by Jove it was very tasty and strong.

And then she would with difficulty and care
Carry each bottle up the steep attic stair
And there it languished for years in the roof
Growing in strength and growing in proof.

When she suddenly died it all went to waste;
Unlabelled bottles nobody dared to taste.
It took my uncles and aunts most of a day
To bring it all down stairs and pour it away.

Oh I can remember that wicked old grin
As we sat and drank a brew she called gin;
High street Granny Barker so long gone
But for me her memory lives on and on.

For me she was one of my very very last
Links with a family lifestyle long past
When life was simpler, possessions few,
And folk didn't complain, just made do.

'Tatie Wine

Our Granny's 'tatie wine
Could blow you off your bike ;
I wobbled off down High Street
To land up in Crossroads dyke
And Big Brother Barry,
Helped pull me out
Then went told our Mam
Who fetched me a clout.

All a little bit older
The very next year
Granny helped us make
Dandelion and nettle beer
Very adventurous
Some of you may think
But just a milky white
Non alcoholic drink.

We kids felt so grown up
As we gathered and stewed
Stirred and boiled up
And finally brewed
Our bucketful of
Sweet liquid
Of very distinctive taste
All drunk long before
Any drop went to waste.

Granny brewed on
Through most of her life
Keeping alive her skills
As a country housewife
And most of them I tried.
But none of them quite like
That old tatie wine that had
Blown me right off my bike.

Mam's Homemade Meat Pie

they come in cardboard boxes
or in clear plastic bag seals
just one of many varieties of
almost instant premade meals
they taste like compressed cardboard
every single one I've ever tasted
every time I've bought one
I've found it money wasted

maybe it's just my memory
but I don't know the reason why
I've never tasted one near as good
as mam's own made meat pie
my mouth has started watering
my taste buds in a state of lust
for her rich brown gravy
and inch thick pastry crust

baked in a huge old pie dish
supported by an egg cup
to let in the air and keep
the crust firmly standing up
she'd no electric cooker
just a little coal fired range
which though so old fashioned
for years she wouldn't change

and you would smell it cooking
the aroma drifting through the air
I didn't need a second shouting
to the table and pull up my chair
we didn't have much money
but there was so much pleasure
eating simple country food
memories I store and treasure

my wife sometimes buys me one
which I pretend to enjoy as I eat
for a kindness is a kindness and
she only does it for a treat
I tell her not to get one too often
but I really don't want to tell her why:
to me they all taste like processed card
after mam's crusty homemade meat pie

On a winter's Saturday night, 1958

The churchyard is different in the dark,
the day time friendly whispering trees
now rearing giant shapes muttering
and chuntering in the night breeze.
The well known tombstones,
regularly lined around,
now seem like teeth
rearing from the ground,
as I make my way quickly,
trying to conceal my fright,
along the path
and through the night.
To lift the stoke hole hatch,
to reveal the concrete stair
leading to the big old furnace
waiting at the bottom there.
Using the shovel blade
I open the black hot door
to shovel the coke quickly
into the small glowing red maw
to heat the church for Sunday
so all are warm sitting there,
after starting their day
with hymns of praise and prayer.
I lift the hatch,

back into the night
eyes still adjusting
from the stoke hole's dim light.
Shapes and sounds assault;
a night owl hoots; walk don't run
back home to our cottage
after a job reluctantly done.
Tomorrow
comes the dawn when
the towering dark shapes
are transformed once again
back to my friendly old trees
that all day long whisper and sing
for me in the constant little breeze.
How can those same boughs
that I love to see and hear,
when it's dark night again
cause in me such an awful fear.

Simple Tastes

I'm searching my supermarket
Though I know it's a waste,
Looking for pickled onions with
That special home made taste;
Like those that Granny Barker made

Firm and plump, white and nice
Floating in their vinegar with
Small gherkin and pickling spice.
Granny Barker had a talent
For pickling then just right.
I can still recall the tang
Of that first bite
When the jar was freshly opened
And declared just ready to eat,
Labelled with Granny's copperplate
Thin and spidery but black and neat.
Brother Barry told me, and he's
Never been known to lie,
They tasted even better with
Granny's Barker's sparrow pie..
Thank the lord that's one of her treats
I don't ever recall being offered to eat!

The death of poor Dicky Bird

Granny barker killed her canary
It wasn't a deliberate act
Though kill him she did
And that's a fact.
She cut poor Dicky's nails

Just a little bit more
Than she should.
He was on the floor
Of his cage
Feet in the air.
Granny said
What's he doing there?
Granddad looked
And Granddad said
Our Dicky's well
And truly dead
And granny cried
And so did I.
We didn't want
Poor Dicky to die.
Granny put the cover
On his cage poor thing
Never again would
We hear him sing.
I'll do me own nails
Granddad said
I don't want to risk
Me waking up dead.

Croftie's Barn

It was a splendid sort of occasion really
As we watched the flames grow higher
On an August day many years past
When Croftie's stacks caught fire

It was the summer holidays
So all the kids were there
Some excitement in the village
Something a little more than rare

The fire engine came fair quick
From a fair few miles away
But water pressure was low
And the hydrant too far away

So they went and slung their hose
In the waters of Brick Field pond
And very soon we realised
How badly we'd been conned

It was a pond without a bottom
For all our lives we'd been told
But very soon its muddy base
Was there to behold

It was touch and go alright
And a fair bit of doubt
But they killed that fire
Before the water ran out

Not before the Dutch barn roof
Exploded with a loud loud bang
Another piece of excitement then
For all our little village gang

Life soon got back to normal
It generally did as a rule
Soon we were all very aware
Of impending return to school

It was a splendid sort of occasion really
As we watched the flames grow higher
On an August day many years past
When Croftie's stacks caught fire

Billy Bulson's Farm

My mam used to clean at Billy Bulson's farm,
A magical place of mystery and charm,
With geese that cackled and hissed and every day.
Without my mam I'd have run away
As they charged with flapping wings.
I was really scared of those fierce big things
With their open beaks and lowered necks.
It really hurt if you got a peck.
But through the flock and into that house of joy
Where I was treated like their own little boy.
A passage was guarded by a stuffed dog fox
Watching the world from his glass walled box.
I knew he watched with his beady eye
And I always walked respectfully by.
Out in the orchard with their daughter Jill,
Amazingly we were never ill,
Stuffing our faces with fruit on the ground
Fallen from the trees growing all around.
Apples and pears and plums and cherries,
In the kitchen garden currants and berries.
Once a week was butter making day.
Mrs Bulson would separate and skim the whey
Then pour the rest in her electric churn
Driven by a rubber belt that made it turn
Producing yellow butter fresh and creamy

I can taste it still - so fresh and dreamy.
She'd shape it all into little square pats
With a pair of special wooden bats
Sometimes there was a little pat for me
To carry it home and eat with our tea.
They still had Shires working on the crops.
Those old boys just never seemed to stop.
I can still feel the thrill deep inside
That first time Billy Bulson let me ride
Holding me on that Shire's back
As it plodded its powerful track
Turning the potatoes out of the land
To be grasped by the picker's hands.
The more they picked the more their pay,
Paid by the bag, not by the day.
Close my eyes and I'm back there still
Guzzling the fruit with my friend Jill
My mam used to clean at Billy Bulson's farm
A magical place of mystery and charm

Bread

Granny Barker mixed dough and put it to rise
Gradually growing miraculously to twice the size
Divide it up and fill each tin
A red hot oven to bake it in

The home made bread that we used to eat
Rarely seen now except as a special treat
The first slice eaten nice and hot
A taste of heaven is what you got
Smothered in butter each loaf so nice
Tasting delicious to the very last slice
Ready watering mouth as you slip it in
Wiping butter drips from off your chin
There's a toast in the fire glowing nice and red
The best toast being made from three day bread
Slathered with butter mixed of course
With liberal slaps of bottled brown sauce
Simple tastes from those days
Simple lives and simple ways
Time quickly changed time moved on
A blink of the eye and many things gone
Life now so much easier but is it as nice
Has progress extracted too great a price

Fields

We used to play in these fields,
acres wide games of hide and seek
that ran and over lapped and spread
over the long green summer weeks
so some times the searcher
and the searched were the same
in the easy ways

of children's games.
We'd play until hunger
or the coming dark
drove us home
from our sprawling park.
In these summer fields year by year
our games broadened and changed
to those of growing girls and boys
and friendships were tested strained
from children to near adults
by new emotions
not easily contained
until the village took control
and we passed to more formal ways
from the easy contacts
of our younger days
and left these fields
and all their joys
to the ones coming behind
still just girls and boys.

Germ Warfare (revisited)

There were those acres of field
Covered each winter by the flood
The rest of the left year fallow
Wet Land not really much good

Except for grazing cattle herds
Or producing some feed hay
At the south end of the village
Seeming almost hidden away
We village children
Could play and roam
Our unknown land
Not far from home
The killer came from Australia
Or so the stories said
Wherever it was the fact was
It left behind its dead
But not a death of any dignity
Blind and swollen eyed
Bloated bodied sitting there
Until they finally died
So deformed
They stank so much
Even our dogs
Wouldn't touch
Introduced deliberately it was said
To clear rabbits from the land
No thought of balance of nature then
That they didn't understand
Just a method of
Laying to rest
One of nature's
Perceived pests

There were certain fields
That particular year
That none of us
Went near
The following summer it was gone
As if it had never been
Apart from small piles of bones
Scattered across the scene

A Special Place

For as long as I can remember
This was a special place to me.
Legs sprawled along the grass
Back against the old oak tree
That had clawed its way, I thought,
To tower miles and miles high.
I could look through its branches
To see framed pieces of the sky.

This was the oak that overhung our roof
Sighed and whispered and chatted away
On and on since ever since I was born
Never silent for very long, night or day
As it played and teased
And worked the breeze
In a chorus with
All the other trees;

Behind me the work noise from uncles shop
Sounds that changed with the time of year
Working blacksmith sounds
Normal and reassuring to hear.
To my left the grave of my granddad
Dead long before his time
Killed by pneumonia
Aged just twenty nine,

Well before I was born.
I hoped he knew it was me there,
Knew I helped my dad each year
With the graveyard's care,
Scything the grass
Carrying it away
To make little piles
To turn to hay

Which dad sold for a few coins
Not enough to pay all his work
But a little extra, a sort of
Seasonal needed perk.
We hoed and shimmed the paths
To give them a cared for aspect.
A gesture from the living
To show the dead respect.

I only remember sunshine
When I visited there
Sunshine and birdsong
And crystal clear air
It was my special place to sit and think
Where I was always at peace and ease,
Amongst the friendly family shades
And my beloved singing talking trees.

Peaceful Place

There was always that air in the village
As if for a little while the place closed down
Curtains closed in respect as the time came
Houses gazing shut eyed the village around
And in the old churchyard the grave tidied
The edges trimmed and turfed and ready
The supports laid across to hold the box
And the bands there to lower it steady
On that last dignified journey into earth
Slowly we returned the broken ground
Tamped and beat it carefully packed
And what was left made the mound
To be grassed then the tributes laid
Flowers and wreaths for all to inspect
The physical manifestation
Of their last respects
Going back to maybe a funeral tea

Usually close enough to walk
Part of the goodbye process
With healing remembering talk
And after due and fitting time
The curtains opened to admit the light
The whole village drawing comfort
From a ritual performed just right
So many many years later
I returned and walked around
Knew the place of every one
I had helped lay in that ground
Felt the calm of that old graveyard
Now just a monument closed at last
Each mound lying sleeping
Under gently waving grass
But cropped so not too long
An eternal release
Under quiet birdsong
Into rest and peace

Saturday night, Yorkshire, 1960

Walking through the village with a pocket full of coins
Anticipation rising, slight tingling in the loins
Catch the bus to Hornsea for the weekly dance,
Where if we're lucky we might stand a chance

Of experiencing a pair of soft female breasts
Press lightly and gently up against our chests.
A lovely heady sensation that just can't last.
I'm sure they make the music end too fast.

Gosh don't all the girls smell nice.
Maybe one will dance with me twice.
More than that, you're going steady
I'm too shy for that – just not ready.
For the last waltz find a special girl
For a slow smoochy fast ending swirl
Then maybe just maybe meet her at the door
And maybe just maybe see her a little more

As you walk her home for that special bliss
Of clutching her tightly in a fumbling kiss;
Only one or two – very seldom any more
Just in case her dad is standing by the door
A possible final peck against the cheek
And a maybe mumbled see you next week
Romantically hoping she'll watch you out of sight
As you wander off into the chilly night.
Can't afford a taxi, last bus long gone,
Five to miles home, I'd better get on.
Sure as Saturday night I'll not be alone
There's always plenty others on the way home
Plenty of laughter, bragging stories and talk
Can make it a pleasant night ending walk.

Oh it was a special living, sixties Yorkshire country days.
Sometime progress throws the wrong things away.

Toast

we'd not many luxuries in life
the one I remember most
was sitting by the fire
turning bread into toast
not the homogenised
standardised loaf of today
but Granny Barker's bread
made the old fashioned way
each slice slathered with butter
which I may have seen turned
bobbing and thickening
as Mrs Bulson churned
nice salty country butter
running from the heat
and to top it off
my very special treat
gobs of brown sauce
to make the taste divine
not to everybody's fancy

but very much to mine
lots of love but no money
lots of warm sensible care
hordes of toast and brown sauce
a mam and dad always there
the wife says I'm just a peasant
and I must say that I agree]
as I eat my special treat
somewhere where she can't see

Village Dance

So many years ago such a long long while
Since I grew up Yorkshire Village style
The Whist Drive finished and all cleared away
Aftermath chatter from those who came to play
French Chalk liberally scattered over the floor
From side to side and right down to the door
It's not quite the Palais but all in all
Not such a bad little village dance hall
Standing in a line best suited stiff and clean
Scarcely daring to move in case you're seen
And all the other boys are feeling the same
All just taking part in the growing up game
Village Hall never seemed so big and wide
Empty floor with lines of us round the side
All the girls in one group, boys in another

All being watched by their relevant mother
The band has set up, bang goes the chance
To escape from this formal social dance
Village occasion held twice or so a year
Most of the residents will be coming here
And not a few from the villages around
New friends made and old ones found
Just a chance before the end of the night
Of the odd bit of aggro and maybe a fight
The odd bloodied nose and lost girl friend
But hands always shaken at the very end
This is the village and the simple life
No fear here of either bottle or a knife
Alliances changing following nature's rule
To bring diversity to the local gene pool
Propriety observed
Decorum every where
Daren't kiss your girl
Cos her mother's there
But in gloom of the Last Waltz's Lowered lights
Long slow smooching is allowed to end the night
So many years ago such a long long while
Since I grew up Yorkshire Village style

chawin' baccy

when it was hot and dusty
working on the farm
and the striking of a match
could cause panic and alarm
when they couldn't smoke
but felt they must
pander a little to
the growing niccy lust

there was chawin' baccy
in a short black stick
very tightly compressed
and not very thick

sliced with a knife
put in the mouth to chaw
filled the niccy lust
made the spittal flow
as a young child
I found it cool and neat
the way they could spit
black juices at their feet
in this modern world
of substance abuse
is chawin' tobaccy
I wonder ever still used

Expansion

There used to be old trees here
Not a wood really just a stand
That straggled and spread across
This then undrained pasture land
That used to partially flood
Nearly every single year
And I would stand with my gun
I suppose just about here
And shoot wild stoggies
And sometimes with luck
The odd rabbit
Or maybe a duck
But not any more
For now it's a street
Trees and land are covered
By both tarmac and concrete
I know the population's grown
And people need their spaces
But do they almost always need
To use those most beautiful places

Great Aunt Ada

Great Aunt Ada
not thought of her for years
she made me laugh
till I cried real tears
fascinated by her talk
never wanting her to go
her every sentence finished
with like and that you know

hidden under the table
her delicious visiting days
mentally counting
each use of her phrase
as she gossiped away
about him and her and so and so
just general village chat
like and that you know

hands over mouth
trying not to laugh aloud
as she chatted away
about the village crowd
such a nice old lady
with a conversational flow
and to emphasise each point
her like and that you know

I don't know why
she came back to mind
I reminisce a lot
these days I find
a horrible child
I hope she didn't know
how I writhed with joy
like and that you know

Memories

when we went to Hull from Withernwick shopping
mother would kick up a fuss
insisting we put on clean underwear
in case we got hit by a bus

I could see the scene in the hospital
I'd be there in a bit of a state
and the nurses and doctors were talking
discussing our various fates

and the nurse would say to the doctor
you know that young lad over there
got hit by a bus while out shopping
but he'd put on his clean underwear

a bright light would flash in heaven

and St Peter would a ring bell
to ensure if I died before morning
I wouldn't be sent down to hell

and God would say to St Peter
you know it does show consideration and care
in case you're hit by a bus while out shopping
to have put on your clean underwear

mother's no longer with us
but to me she'll always be there
for her love and kindness and compassion
and her views on clean underwear

Conversations

Conversations with my father
Bittersweet and maybe sad
Conversations with my father
Talks that we never had
Companionably silent
As we set off walking
Neither of us known
For doing too much talking
Down Lambwath road
To Billy Bulson's farm
Each with a broken 12 bore

Tucked safely underarm
I was at his hospital bedside
On the day that he died
Only alone in the car
Did I give in and cry
I am just about that age
And like him slowing down
Maybe that's the reason now
I feel him there and around
We talk about the garden
Always his joy and pride
He was never the man
To spend his time inside
We talk of this and that
In our lazy easy way
And I suppose we chat now
Nearly every single day
Maybe it's because I'm older
That much nearer the other end
But there we sit and chat
Like two good old friends
Conversations with my father
Bitter sweet and maybe sad
Conversations with my father
Talks I wish we'd really had

Emily Medforth - village School Teacher

I thought she was old when I saw her,
Ancient to me only just reached four.
I remember still those feelings as mam
Presented me to her at the old school door.
She never grew any older.
Just never seemed to age.
Never treated us unfairly.
Never punished us in rage.
Just expected us to follow the rules
To be quiet and good and obey,
Then go home quietly and discreetly
At the end of another school day.
We were all taught our places
In a world of black and white.
She read my first faltering poetry
Encouraged me to write,
To do my best
In life's race
But to never never
Forget my place.
She lived to over 90 years
Then suddenly was gone
Never changing her standards
In a world that had fast moved on.
I don't think any of us ever thanked her

For guiding us as we grew,
But most of us were grateful
And I'm certain sure she knew.
She was there when we scattered dad's ashes
Over Granny and Granddad Barker's grave
I think she nodded slightly to
My acknowledging wave:
But she didn't look any older
Maybe she'd grown a little small
Or maybe over the passing years
It was me who'd grown too tall.

Floods

Every winter Lambwaths flooded
Breaching stream banks either side
So there was a stretch of water
Maybe fifty yards or so wide
And the Buttercup meadows in which
We used to play, dance, chase, leap
Were now knee high covered
With a cold watery deep
A sort of shimmering expanse
Of rippling shifting grey white
Under winter's stars or when
Reflecting winter moonlight

It washed away all the little bones
The year the rabbit plague struck
Or covered them decently with
Its flow of oozy muddy muck
It was good to walk down there
In that cold quiet dark land
Fields as welcoming and familiar
As the back of my own hand
Each winter in its time passed
And the floods long gone down
Lambwaths became once more
The village's lush green playground

village churchyard

the gates are unlocked always
for this place belongs to all

there are rows of standing stones
which church goers walk through
some are centuries old
some by comparison quite new
some are so weathered
the names can't be read
I wonder if the loss of the name
makes them any more dead
this is the stone of an uncle
though we never met

because at the time he died
I wasn't been born yet
and my aunt lies with him
both their names are clear
though she didn't join him
for more than thirty years

other family lies here
in unmarked mounds
which over time have sunk
to near level with the ground
I don't often visit them
for to be honest I find
they are so much more real
just kept here in my mind

very little has changed
except the trees are less
and the passing of years
no longer brings me distress
this is such a peaceful place
with its rows of standing stones
relentlessly guarding
those mouldering old bones

and the gates are always unlocked
for all to wander around in peace

Summer Childhood

We would swing from the old oak
On lengths of old wagon rope
Slung from a high branch,
The seat made from old sacks
That rubbed and wore against
Young bare legs as we clung
With excited screams as we seemed
To rise higher and higher
Pushed faster and harder towards
That always blue blue sky glimpsed
Between the swaying sighing leaves
Until tired of this fun
We browsed the old orchard
Eating the windfall fruit
Competing with the yellow wasps
And bees and flies
For the sweet plums damsons
Apples pears and then maybe
To the kitchen garden to sample
Strawberries gooseberries currants
Both red and black sweet raspberries
Then maybe a little afternoon nap
Before returning to the old oak
For one last swing before home
Holding mams hand along the lane
Leaving Billy Bulson's farm behind

For the old cottage beneath the trees
Overhanging from the old churchyard
To eat and play and sleep safely
Until the next say when mam
Returned there to work
And I returned to play
Passing happy long green summers
Until I eased into the shock of life

Summer circa 1953

The long branches of Weeping Willow
Stretched down as though to sweep
The grass of the of the big front lawn
Where the Old Vicarage seemed to sleep
The overhang forming an enclosed
Almost complete cool green tent
Where on those long summer's days
Some of us younger boys went
To chat and play
Blissfully unaware
Our noise told all
Just where we were
Calmed by the breeze shaken leaves
Our own little world of filtered light
Curtained enclosed secured
Away from adult sight

Many plans being planned
Many dreams being dreamed
Much mischief's thought of
Many schemes being schemed
In a sort of stillness
Of soft leafy sighs
As long afternoons
Crept deliciously by
Until the maybe evening hunger
Sent us scurrying home one by one

And the old Weeping Willow settled
To peaceful sleep with its charges gone
And maybe the Old Vicarage checked
To see all was safe secure and right
Before it and the old Weeping Willow
Settled down to a warm and peaceful night

Rough shooting 3

Dad would head shoot mallard
in full flight
bring them down
from the sky at night.
He used a twelve bore
with full pellet spread,

but seldom the body,
mostly the head.
Scarcely a pellet to ruin the meat,
shot for all our family to eat

It was on a big old Fordson Major
that dad took his driving test
after months of patient practise
to pass it or do his level best.
Came the day, he failed.
Poorish eyesight.
Very annoyed
until that very night;
trying to get a brace of geese
with just one shot
but it wasn't geese
that he got.
A pair of swans came crashing down
Dead before they hit the ground.

He laid them for a dog fox to get,
By placing them atop his set.
Shooting swans is against the law,
but what worried dad even more
he mistook them for geese that awful night:
And he could head shoot a mallard in flight.

It was on the same old tractor
Dad took his second test

With his new glasses
He could drive like the best.
After months at long last
he was legal 'cos he passed.
Dad could head shoot a mallard in full flight
bring them down from the sky at night,
and not the very least
he could once again
tell the swans from the geese.

1957

1957 was the year
When the sap started to rise.
We saw our contemporary girls
Change shape before our eyes.
They seemed to get rounder
And we could see on each chest
The gentle little outlines of
Slowly budding breasts.
And some of our mixed games
We no longer played very much
For it was no longer allowed
To wrestle and to touch.
And they seemed to change
As changeable as the weather
No longer mixed groups but

Mainly just the girls together.
And we boys struggled
With teenage spotty faces
And embarrassment of hair
Growing in once bare places.
And at times the problems,
And at times the shame
Of testosterone moods though
We didn't ever know the name.
The older boys' jokes
And growing up fears
Yes 1957 was, all in all
Quite an eventful year.

Hornsea, 1954

They played the National Anthem,
God Save the Queen,
As the final credits rolled
Down the big silver screen.
Quite a few stood to attention
While quite a few more
Pushed their way past
And made for the door.

Outside in the street
We did the Duke Wayne Walk

And chattered to ourselves
With our Duke Wayne talk.
And I climbed a lamp post
And mam clouted my ear.
And one of the other lads
Gave a little cheer.

So we had a little scuffle,
Couldn't be called a fight,
As we walked to the bus
From our rare cinema night.
Mam was complaining
How rude they'd all been
To rush for the door
During God Save the Queen.

One of the other's mams said she
Didn't think the Queen would care
Cos she heard it so often
And she wasn't even there.
The warm bus ride home,
That rare and special treat,
All huddled up together
On the upstairs big back seat.

conflicts

When I went to school in the city
my friends though I was poor,
but I didn't understand
wasn't really very sure;
I only knew that
when I got home
I had all those miles
of fields to roam,
and every long summer
within easy reach,
half hour's walk,
was Cowden beach.
They may have had running water
and toilets that flushed
but I hated their streets
their lives that rushed.
I was never ever at ease
when I was there,
hated the noise,
the very air.
They had the cinemas,
I had the sun.
They could play in the parks
I could walk with my gun;
and very special, I had two lives.
My friends known almost from birth

village folk with families like mine
mostly living from and with the earth
and my newly found city friends.
I kept each in their own part of my day
the best of both worlds,
I liked it that way.
A man's not poor
if he needs to be told
what he's missing
out there in the cold
My life may have been considered lacking
by those friends back there in the city,
from my position it was they
who needed my pity.

Just A Box Of Old Photos

Just a box of old photos on my desk for twenty years.
Pull one out from anywhere and a memory appears.
When Uncle Joe died
Aunt Elsie really tried
She had always lived in his shade
And very soon she began to fade

I visited as often as I could

But with my own family problems
Not as often as I should
We tried to talk tried to fill the gaps
But most times our chat would lapse
I hope she drew comfort from my just being there
I hope I didn't show I needed to be elsewhere
When I cleared her house I found
This battered old biscuit tin
With all these photos
Just thrown in
Saw the little girl
Slowly grow
To the beautiful woman
Who captured Joe
Saw my village peopled
But such a shame
No one left now
Knows their names
I think of the fun we should have had
Aunt Elsie and me
Could have filled all the hours
That old box on her knee
Picking faces telling shames
Telling all the fun and games
No conversation dragging
Hoping she didn't know
As soon as I could
I wanted to go

I really believe we are never truly dead
So long as our picture's there in someone's head:
It's not really that much of a shame
If they cant recall our name.
That old box of photos looked at a little nearly every day
That old box of photos that will never again be shut away

Uncle Wilf

He'd long ago shoed his last horse,
A hunter that kicked him to the floor
And, no longer being a young man,
Didn't want such work anymore.
For they were young and fretful,
Not so easy to command,
Not like the gentle cart horse
That would patiently stand
So solid and tall, almost
Reaching up to the roof,
Balancing three legged as he
Shoed each individual hoof.
For years he mended Binders
Hooped wooden cart wheels
Exercised his hard won skIll

Working both iron and steel;
But the Combine took over,
Work became a bit more rare
Not really so much need then to
Have a blacksmith always there.
New machinery didn't need mending,
He wouldn't have known where to start,
They just went to the company store
And replaced the failed part.
So the forge went cold
As he decided to retire
No more working chats
Around its cheerful fire;
The hooping ring overgrown
The Smithy yard covered in weed
As Docks and Dandelions
Thrived and spread their seed.
The old wooden doors padlocked
And with the Yard emptied at last
The role of village blacksmith
Became just a thing of the past.
The forge still stands, protected,
Rebuilt and externally restored.
Does it echo of farmers chatter
As the fire crackles and roars.
Do blows from the hammer
Vibrate and ring
Does the worn old anvil

In response sweetly sing.
Does the shade of Uncle Wilf
At the start of every working day
Saunter across his crowded yard
To get his Forge fired and under way.

Frikkies And Fries

At about the age of 50 I discovered the Mosel Valley and another village nestled on its banks, and for 15 years or so it became a special place for me and my late wife. We made wonderful friends there, watched their children grow and enjoyed being a part of their family. Since my wife's death I have not been able to return there. It was our special place.

Now I have a new, equally happy, but very different life, and one day I may be able to return there.

Cochem
Picking Grapes
Old Bielstein
Frikkies and Fries
Kaffee Lang
Reisling Dernst
Steinaeger
Trier
Reisling
Reisling ii
Rathaus Strasse
Mosel Valley
Mosel River
Mosel River ii
Father Mosel
Special Mornings

Cochem

Overlooked by its castle
Standing on the high ground
Keeping a peaceful eye
On that little Mosel town,
Whose two halves
Lie on opposing sides
Of the Mosel River,
Split by a giant's stride.

And the little Ice Cream Cafe,
Where the selection is so good,
Can be feet under water
When that River is in flood.
But the little town of Cochem
With its narrow shopping streets
And its little cafe bars
Where neighbours often meet,

Is so human in size,
Moving at its leisurely pace,
And to this village born man
Is perhaps my perfect place.
There I can watch the river

As I drink my glass of Pils
And for a while forget
The world and all its ills. Cochem

Overlooked by its castle
Standing on the high ground
Keeping a peaceful eye
On that little Mosel town,
Whose two halves
Lie on opposing sides
Of the Mosel River,
Split by a giant's stride.
And the little Ice Cream Cafe,
Where the selection is so good,
Can be feet under water
When that River is in flood.
But the little town of Cochem
With its narrow shopping streets
And its little cafe bars
Where neighbours often meet,

Is so human in size,
Moving at its leisurely pace,
And to this village born man
Is perhaps my perfect place.

There I can watch the river
As I drink my glass of Pils
And for a while forget
The world and all its ills.

Picking Grapes

Mosel river meanders
On its deep cut line
Flowing through its valley
On to join the Rivet Rhine.
He is fast and he is dangerous,
At times treacherous, always deep,
Yet seems to flow sedately
As though he were asleep.

Vines march down hillsides
Almost down to his banks
Standing at attention in
Long luscious green ranks,
And we picked the grapes
On that long sloping hill
Vertigo and tiredness
Overcome by power of will.

Sweet juicy Rieslings but
No time or energy to waste
No time just to suck one
And enjoy that sugary taste.
Up and down , up and down
Reach, pull, pick Bunches of green
Trying to keep a rhythm
A human picking machine.

And the feeling of relief
When the picking came to end
And the grassy bank to rest on
A softly cushioned green friend.
It eased the aching muscles
At the end of a hard day
While down below the Mosel
Swept serenely on his way.

On a different scale
To the human span
Maybe blithely unaware
Of the existence of any man.
Through the castled hillsides
On his waving deep cut line
Until he reaches Koblenz
To join the mighty River Rhine.

Old Bielstein

This is my place of peace
The place that I hope to die
Beside the whispering Mosel
Under a blue Mosel sky.

Not soon, not for many years yet,
So I can wander these quiet lanes
Watching Mosel grapes
Washed by Mosel rains;
Then with the late sunshine
Burst into sweetness and taste
So that a year's labour
Has not gone to waste.
So we sit in old Bielstein
To often take a quiet glass

And watch the flowing river
As the hours gently pass;
Maybe a cake at the castle
Whose ruins dominate the hill,
Scene of so much history
Yet standing there still.

And over all this place
Such a feeling of peace
That I feel contentment,
Fulfilled and at my ease.

A stroll back by the river
For a pleasant day's end,
Good food and company
With my good Mosel friends.

Frikkies And Fries

Frikkies and Fries in Cochem,
Just off the town square,
Washed down with a cold Pils,
Breathing clear Mosel air.
Such a very pleasant place
Relaxed and sitting down
Taking in the beauty of
This very ancient town.

This town of changing allegiance,
This town of chequered past,
Now settled in place again,
As part of Germany at last.
Buildings ancient or restored,

Like the Old Mustard Mill
Now a tourist attraction
But a working building still,

Nudge and nestle to the river,
No sign of damage from a war
That almost killed a town, damaged
To an extent never seen before.
This is a pleasant little place
Where I feel so at ease
To stroll gently around
To do just as I please.

A stroll down the hill
The Mosel in full view
To check the ice parlour
For what flavours are new.
Every visit there brings
Such pleasant tasty surprise
That just adds to the joy of
Spicy Frikkies and crispy Fries.

Kaffee Lang

It clicks and it whirs and it chunters,
This wonderful little machine,
As it takes and measures and grinds
Those marvellous little brown black beans.
It hisses and it gurgles and it splutters
Then finally begins to pour
And just seconds later
A Kaffee Lang awaits once more,
Which just slips down the throat
So any morning muzziness slips away;
After such a fine coffee
A man can face any day.f

Reisling-Dernst

Mosel Wein for sweetness
At the day's end
Mosel Wein to enjoy
Just chatting with friends

It stands on the table
This very special Wein

Last years grapes that
I helped strip from their vine;
Saw them carried up the hill,
Some glistening and wet,
A mixture of pressure ooze
And maybe picker's sweat.

I followed them to the Wein Haus,
Saw them pumped tumbling and loose
Into the first pressure tank,
Tasted their first sweet juice,
Ate the barbecued meat served
At the end of the picking day
Breathed in Mosel air
As we chatted the night away.

Now just one year later
We meet up again
And that bottle soon will be
Another of my life's dead men
It stands on the table
I will not drink it in haste
For I want to slowly savour
That very special first taste

Mosel Wein for sweetness
At the day's end
Mosel Wein to enjoy
Just chatting with friends

Steinaeger

I used to call her Frau Fankel,
I never did know her real name.
We stayed with her on the Mosel
That very first time we came;
And I told her how in Effeld
We played the dice game Snake Eyes
With, just for ease of choice,
Steinaeger as the loser's prize.

I told her more of Steinaeger,
That drink I remembered so well,
With its sort of oily appearance
And taste of its own as well.
Frau Fankel produced a dusty bottle
From the depths of a cold drinks drawer
And I was face to face with my nemesis
A bottle of Steinaeger once more.

I tossed a full measure down,
Really in a panicky haste,
And felt in my throat once more
That guts wrenching and dreadful taste.
I washed my mouth out very quickly
With a good measure of cold Pilsner beer
Before bowing so slowly to Frau Fankel
And she and the staff gave a cheer.

For a dare is a dare is a dare
And here up in Yorkshire we say
About your money and your mouth
And I reckon that's still my way.
As for that long past experience,
My memory had served me so well
For that little local schnapps drink
Still tasted a mouthful from hell.

Trier, Summer 2001

I sat in this public square
just to rest my aching feet.
This couple wandered up
sat next to me on the seat.

To say they were elderly
is just my vanity;
In truth they can't have been
very much older than me.
My command of the language
is a long standing joke
so I panicked a little bit
when the woman spoke;
For she used a country dialect
and I had my Yorkshire twang
yet somehow the conversation
cheerfully chugged along.
By speaking slowly and carefully,
with nods and use of our hands
we managed to chat away
and each seemed to understand
what the other was talking about.
We were all happily chatting away
like three old army mates
on a re- union day.
A pleasant half hour passed
then we shook hands all three
when it was time for me to go.
This just seems to prove to me
It's your manner and attitude,
not so much what you say
that really counts
at the end of the day:

And it helps once in a while
to just sit there and smile.

Reisling

You hide there away from me
As though I intended rape
But I'll have you in my bucket
You little elusive grape.

That's my first one filled,
Right up to the lip
And placed in the line
For Christian to tip.

I think an early finish,
Rather than a late,
If we continue picking
Grapes at this rate.

The day has got hotter
Since the mist has broken
As for the early finish
I wish I'd never spoken

For this gentle wine berg
Suddenly seems so very steep
And I think I'll pick grapes
Tonight all through my sleep.

And next time I open a bottle
I'll take some time to think
About the love and effort gone
In growing grapes for drink.

They hid away from me
As though I'd intended rape,
But I got them in my bucket
Those sweet elusive grapes

Reisling ii

Mosel wine is sweet,
Taken in little sips,
Smell that aroma,
As glass approaches lips.

The barbecue is lit and stoked
With dried vine wood

That slowly evenly burns
Giving a layer that is good,
(Better than any charcoal)
At giving off the right heat
To do justice to the quality
Of our vast array of meat.

We are lounging in the garden
Each sprawled in their chair
Drinking Pils in bottles
In the mild September air.
We have picked the grapes
And taken them to the press;
Maybe four thousand litres
Of new wine, more or less.

And we are sitting at the table
At the end of working day.
A time of relaxing talk.
A time of relaxing play.
And the aroma from the grill'
As it comes and goes,
Driven by the breeze,
Plays such tricks with the nose

It's that time of the day
That I think I like the best
Full of banter and good chat
As we take our well earned rest.
Appetites are rising;
Two minutes more at least
Before food is at the table
And its time to take the feast.

Mosel wine is sweet
Taken in little sips
Smell that aroma
As glass approaches lips

rathaus strasse 8

up the wendel treppe
that little spiral stair
to the sleeping platform
snugly built there
open the roof window
breathe the pure clear
air listen to the river
that calls me back here
mosel valley magic

mosel sweet wine
mosel dear friends
in this paradise of mine

Mosel Valley – August 2010

The village lies unchanged like an ancient peaceful sleeper
though perhaps this year the hills seem a little steeper
and I know with the usage my legs will get stronger
but my exploring walks seem to take a little bit longer.
The vines march up the slopes, almost touchingly near
but in my heart I know I'll not help picking them this year.
I sit in the night with those dear friends of mine
enjoying the chat and the sweet Mosel wine.

And I want every moment seared in my brain
because just maybe I'll not be here again,

for that long road of life which seemed to extend
on and on forever now seems to have an end.
So I start to look at things through very different eyes
as I enjoy my village under warm Mosel skies
while the river, as ever, rolls on and on and on its way
supremely unaware of one man and his short short stay.

Mosel River

Mosel River flows fast and wide and deep
Down it's valley of hoarded grape vines
Seen from the water bus that takes us
Sedately towards those friends of mine.
I can feel the excitement rise as every
Stop brings us nearer the village where,
For just a few days I will re- discover
All the things that year after year
Call me ever more strongly there.
This village is old, yet growing
Gently, I see the growth as I stroll
As I do the every first morning,
Playing my new visitor role,

Through the old streets around
The old original village walls.
I see even the smallest of changes
For in my mind I remember it all
As it was even as I see it as it is.
Down Rathaus Strasse and I hear
Those special sounds that tell me
The River Mosel is now so near;
Today she is flowing gently contained,
But Monica has pictures of its floods;
Many feet under water this very spot
Where I am now am so casually stood
Watching the barges enter the locks
Through the gates and on they go
Up and down this busy river
In an almost constant flow.
I watch this river.
I feel its peace.
I am home.
I am at ease.
Mosel River flows fast and wide and deep
Down it's valley of hoarded grape vines
Seen from the water bus that takes me
Sedately towards those friends of mine

Mosel River ii

Mosel River keeps on flowing
In its own steady way.
I watch it for a while
Nearly every here day.
The vines stand in rows
Reaching down the hill,
A regiment of greenery
Parade ground still.

Herr Dernst sits in Mesenich,
The centre of his clan;
Each year I pay respects
To this well respected man.

Monica's laughter flows around,
A dear friend always there
In this place we all love
This very special somewhere.

Franz makes me welcome,
A companion as well as friend.
Together we've talked to
Many a wine bottle's end.

Jacqueline is in America
Happily married to her John,
But I still see her in my mind
So she's not really gone.
Marcel is near full grown;
Christian a young man now;
The years have flown away,
I don't know where or how.

The breeze down the valley
Makes me feel a little colder.
I know where those years have gone.
I've grown just that much older.
I watch it for a while
Nearly every here day;
Mosel River keeps on flowing
In its own steady way.

Father Mosel

Mosel Valley called me back
Big Silver bird took me there
Winged me through the miles
Saw Mosel River from the air
Felt the pull felt the call

On Hunsruck ground
Sat in the car
Looked all around
Landscapes remembered
Mosel Valley drawing near
First glimpse of Mosel River
Then Father Mosel I am here
No tension
At peace
Father Mosel
Brings release

I picked your grapes From the vine
After a glass Of last year's wine
Fingers rich With the taste
Licked free of juice None gone to waste
If I still live I will be here
For my harvest 's wine This time next year
No tension At peace
Father Mosel   Brings release

Mosel Valley calls me back
I can hear you it seems
Talking gently to me
In my waking dreams
Mosel Valley call me back
Big Silver bird will take me there
Wing me through the miles

Smell Mosel Valley clean clear air
No tension
At peace
Father Mosel
Brings release

Special Mornings

So many special mornings
Seeing the fret clear off the hills
To reveal clear blue skies.
The vines in lines up the slopes
Like regiments at ease.
One year we helped pick them,
Working up and down the rows
Cutting bunches into buckets
Emptied into the back pack
For Chris to empty them juicy
Green into the trailer ready
To be hauled to the vintner, who
Because I was a visitor
Showed me around, pressing
Samples of wine for me to taste
So I rode back on thr tractor
Just a little squiffy, and the
Next year drinking the wine
From those grapes we'd picked.

So many special days there
With special friends
In that special place.
Our special place.
Now that I am alone
I need to go back just once more
To say thank you
And goodbye.
This special place both loved
And shared that I cannot face
More than once without her.
I did not know I could experience
And bear such despair.
So many of the past months
Just blurred memories
When I doubted my sanity.
So I keep those mornings
I'm my mind and cry inside
While smiling to the world,
For appearances must be kept,
And grief be suffered silently
To allow others
To get on living their lives,
And for me to just exist.

All poems in this book are subject to © Terry Ireland 2017

ALL RIGHTS RESERVED

This book contains material protected under Copyright Laws. Any unauthorised reprint or use of this material is prohibited. No part of this book may be reproduced or transmitted in any form or by any means, including photocopying, recordng or by any information storage and retrieval system withour express written permission from the author.